Jo[...]

Abolition!

Newton, the ex-slave trader, and
Wilberforce, the little liberator

© The Trinity Forum, P.O. Box 9464, McLean, Virginia 22102-0464 USA
This UK edition © by Day One Publications 2007
First printed 2007

ISBN 978-1-903087-99-2

9 781903 087992

ISBN 978-1-903087-99-2

British Library Cataloguing in Publication Data available

Published by Day One Publications
Ryelands Road, Leominster, HR6 8NZ
☎ 01568 613 740 FAX 01568 611 473
email—sales@dayone.co.uk
web site—www.dayone.co.uk
North American—e-mail—sales@dayonebookstore.com
North American—web site—www.dayonebookstore.com

Designed by Kathryn Chedgzoy and printed by Gutenberg Press, Malta

Contents

This bicentennial salute to the abolition of the slave trade in 1807 by the British Parliament, and by the United States Congress, is a joint enterprise by myself and the John Newton Project. JNP's co-founder, Marylynn Rouse, furnished transcripts of manuscripts from an archive which was closed when I was researching my *Wilberforce* in the 1970s but is now in the public domain, with other material found by her in archives or private ownership in Britain and North America, and I am most grateful for her collaboration in this and other ways.

The John Newton Project is bringing together in a multi-volume series on their website, www.johnnewton.org, all that John Newton wrote, whether published or unpublished.

The salute is mainly drawn or condensed from my full-length biography *Wilberforce* (Constable 1977) and my shorter *Amazing Grace: John Newton's Story* (Hodder 1981). Both books are still in print, the current editions being by Kingsway. Readers who want the story in the round, and especially how it led on to emancipation and Wilberforce's many other achievements, should consult these two books.

John Pollock

Abolition! 5

Some terms explained

merchantman	a merchant ship
bosun	[in the 18th-century Royal Navy] the senior non-commissioned (petty) officer in charge of crew and sails, etc., to carry out the orders of the captain and the lieutenant
middle passage	the sea journey undertaken by slave ships from West Africa to the West Indies
factory	[in slave-trading context] an establishment for traders carrying on business in a foreign country
factor	a merchant buying and selling on commission

The passage of a bill through Parliament:

An MP proposing a new law (a *motion*) must obtain leave of the House of Commons to bring in a *bill*. He presents his bill briefly (the *first reading*) and the Speaker of the House orders it to be printed and fixes a date for the *second reading*, the main debate. Then each member who is in the Chamber, or can reach the lobby in time, votes 'Aye' or 'No'. If 'the Ayes have it', the bill goes to Committee for detailed discussion, amendments, etc. Witnesses may be examined at 'the bar of the House' (i.e. outside the Chamber) by lawyers (*counsel*).

The Committee reports at the *third reading*. If the bill is passed it goes to the Lords (the Upper House) where it is either rejected or returned to the Commons with or without amendments.

When the bill is finally accepted by both Houses, it receives the Royal Assent and becomes an *Act of Parliament*.

Wimbledon, 1769

A small boy aged ten was playing in the grounds of his uncle's pleasant, rural villa on the edge of Wimbledon Common, in the summer of 1769, when the family carriage drew up at the door.

The boy ran to greet his uncle. They were both named William Wilberforce. Uncle William stepped down, a little stiff from the seven-mile drive into the country from his fine London house overlooking Green Park. With a friendly face and sparkling eyes, he was in his late forties but had retired early from his business as a merchant in Hull to enjoy his wealth and pursue good causes.

As the nephew reached the carriage door, the uncle was helping down his guest. Young William saw a clergyman, also in his forties. He was not in clerical dress but wore his sea-captain's jacket. He was rather small and bandy-legged, as so many seamen were, and had a weather-beaten face. It seemed to blend a strong determination with a kind and merry heart. As the uncle introduced the

Wilberforce, aged 11. Portrait by John Russell, 1770

Reverend John Newton, the boy felt at once that here was a man he could trust.

The beloved Aunt Hannah had come to the door, on hearing the carriage, to greet their great friend John Newton, parson of Olney in Buckinghamshire. Her half-brother John Thornton, a director of the

William and Hannah Wilberforce, portrait in the Wilberforce House Museum

Russia Company and vastly rich, had come to deep faith through George Whitefield and loved to support evangelical clergymen: he gave an annual stipend to Newton to spend on hospitality and on relief to the poor in his parish.

They all went indoors, and Newton could admire the murals on the staircase and the ceiling by Angelica Kauffman, the young Swiss-born artist who had just been nominated a Royal Academician, a foundation member of the new Royal Academy.

Master Wilberforce quickly became devoted to the sea-captain-turned-parson, and he to William for his cheerful disposition and wit, and for his musical treble (later the pleasing tenor that delighted London society when he entered Parliament). Newton had just been given use of the great room of Olney's unoccupied mansion where a hundred and thirty people could sing and pray with more freedom than in the parish church. He had already written hymns and found out tunes. Man and boy sang together his new hymn: *How Sweet the Name of Jesus Sounds*.

The boy's father had died the previous year. His mother, then in poor health and grieving for the loss of her husband and her elder daughter, had accepted the offer of her brother-in-law and his childless wife to bring up William, who thus left Hull for Wimbledon and met John Newton in the summer of 1769.

1769 was the year that the Duke of Wellington and Napoleon were born. It was the year of the great Bengal famine, the invention of the spinning jenny and the discovery and naming of San Francisco Bay. But it was a year, too, when thousands of African men, women and children were transported across the Atlantic as black cargo, packed in comparatively small ships, to a lifetime of hard labour as slaves in the West Indies or the American mainland.

The slave trade was one of the anchors of the British economy. As Hull was not a slave port, and the Wilberforce wealth came from the Baltic trade, young William would not have been aware of it, though he would have seen a few black boys, in their masters' liveries, running errands when he stayed in his uncle's London house.

His new friend the Reverend Mr Newton, on the other hand, was thoroughly aware of it. He may have told exciting tales of slaves on his ships who furiously attempted to regain their freedom, for although he had come to hate the distasteful occupation of his earlier years he had not yet discovered that this legal and respected trade was criminal.

No one in 1769 would have foreseen that these two, John Newton and William Wilberforce, of different generations and thirty-four years apart in age, would be the key characters in the story of the abolition of the slave trade in 1807: outlawed by the British Parliament and in the United States Congress.

And though the parson may have shown the boy the marks where heavy fetters had chafed his wrists, he certainly would not have displayed the scars on his back.

I believed my own lie and like an unwary sailor who quits his port just before a rising storm, I renounced the hopes and comforts of the gospel at the very time when every other comfort was about to fail me.

Newton, recalling 1744

Flogged

On 1 March 1744, Captain Philip Carteret of the Royal Navy, commanding HMS *Harwich* in the lower Thames, awaiting the declaration of war with France, sent out a press gang. Its lieutenant had the legal right to press any seaman into the navy unless the man was already serving on a merchantman and produced a 'certificate of protection' signed by his ship's master. One of those pressed that morning was the eighteen-year-old John Newton.

He sent a desperate note to his father, a captain in the Mediterranean trade who was now a senior official of the Royal Africa Company. But the lieutenant respectfully refused to release a likely lad who had been trained by his own father. John's lack of a protection proved disastrous.

The horrors John knew by hearsay now had to be tasted to the full—the physical and mental strain of working the ship in all weathers, the dread of corporal punishment, the close confinement with three hundred men, the coarseness and debauchery. Newton lessened his own swearing and attempted to live cleanly, if only to display that he was neither jailbird nor lout but a sea captain's son.

And the sea captain's influence was strong enough to persuade Captain Carteret to promote Newton to the quarterdeck as a midshipman.

Born in 1725, Newton had been a child of two worlds, rather terrified of his father, yet thrilled to be taken over his ship when it was anchored near their home in Wapping, east of the Tower of London. He adored his mother, Elizabeth, and loved to attend her chapel and sing the hymns, and to listen to her stories about Jesus as she lay coughing on her bed, for she was already in an advanced state of tuberculosis. The captain planned for him to be a sea officer. She wanted him to go to university and then to an academy for preachers.

Her influence filtered deeper into his soul than he could realize. But when he was seven her great friend Elizabeth Catlett, wife of a customs officer in Chatham, took her home so that John should not see her die.

More than six months later, in the spring of 1733, Captain Newton returned to find himself a widower, and he promptly married again. John became a rather unwanted stepson, living with his stepmother and, in time, two half-brothers, on her parents' farm in Essex at Aveley, close to the northern bank of the lower Thames. On his eleventh birthday, his father took him to sea, 'a little sailor boy', carrying a cargo of corn to the Mediterranean. The captain cushioned him from the crew yet imposed a strict discipline which, on this and five more voyages over the next six years, gave him a solid grounding in seamanship and hardened his body. At sea, and at Aveley between voyages, he grew into a youth of mixed character: impulsive yet dreamy; a great reader yet a leader in mischief; sometimes religious, at other times not.

Captain Newton, on retiring from the sea, bought a house at Rotherhithe, close to London Pool, and placed John as third mate under another Mediterranean captain, who reported that this dreamy lad would never make an officer worthy of the Newton name. So he wrote to a close friend, the Liverpool ship-owner Joseph Manesty, who had interests in slaves and sugar in Jamaica. Manesty promised to make John's fortune. Captain Newton had never been involved in the slave trade, but like almost every Englishman of the day he accepted it as vital to national prosperity.

A few days before John was due to take ship for Jamaica, a letter from Chatham arrived. On breaking the seal he recognized the name of Elizabeth Catlett, his mother's dearest friend in whose house she had died. Mrs Catlett had not approved of the hasty remarriage of Captain Newton, and the two families had severed relations; but no doubt she had promised her dying friend to remember her son, since the two of them had lightly plotted that Elizabeth Newton's John should grow up to marry Elizabeth Catlett's Mary ('Polly'), who was now nearly fourteen. Mrs Catlett invited him to stay should he ever be near Chatham.

She had waited ten years. She had chosen the moment when he was to disappear for a prolonged absence overseas. Her invitation reached him when he was about to ride into her part of Kent on an errand for his father.

Yet when John reached the turn on his homeward journey on 12 December 1742, only the prospect of a hot meal by the fire made him dismount at their door. It was opened by a girl who had to be Polly. Her mother ran forward and kissed her old friend's features that she saw in his face, and told him to stay as long as he liked.

Polly seemed different from any other girl. Bashful, well grown, with a dimple and a smile, her kindness and simplicity drew him until only good breeding stopped him calling her, then and there, 'My dearest, sweetest dear Polly.' She was not a great beauty. She was less intelligent than he, wrote in an awkward, rounded hand and could not spell. She sang sweetly, loved opera tunes and could command the obedience and affection of the younger Catletts. Innocence and purity were self-evident, but she enjoyed a frolic and laughter. Newton, at seventeen, fell head over heels in love.

He could not declare his love, being an almost penniless youth. He swore to himself he would make a fortune to throw at her feet, yet he could not bear to leave her. Three days passed like a dream. A fourth, and still Newton stayed. The Catletts, unaware that he was bound for Jamaica, did not hurry him to saddle his horse. Love-crazed, he lingered until the West India ship must have sailed, while his father and stepmother were miserable, thinking he had been murdered by a highwayman or, more likely, taken by the navy's press gang.

He rode home after three weeks. The captain received him in anger, but forgave quickly, having secretly regretted that his son would have ceased to be a seaman. For punishment, he had to sail a voyage as a common sailor. John thought it a small price for the hope of seeing Polly again within the year.

The ten-month voyage taught him to step lively, haul on the capstan singing the shanties, and eat hardtack instead of captain's bread. He smoked a clay pipe, swore with the best, swapped bawdy stories, yet, unlike the other sailors, still kept himself from women. At the age of eighteen, he rated sexual immorality the ultimate sin, so he did not follow his friends into brothels.

And Polly held his heart.

His father next obtained him an officer's berth on a merchantman. With Britain on the verge of war with France, John had to keep a sharp watch and avoid the press gang until he joined his ship and received his protection. However, he might ride down to the Catletts for a few days after Christmas. John could not bear to leave Polly. Once again, irresponsible and ungrateful, he overstayed his leave, missed his ship and returned to an irate parent.

His father nearly threw him over, but relented. Before the captain had found him another ship, the Newtons went down to the Essex farm. John crossed the Thames to visit Polly, and walked straight into the press gang from HMS *Harwich*, to endure the misery of those first weeks on the lower deck until his father's intervention.

Newton's sudden promotion to the quarterdeck, as midshipman, brought out the worst in him. He resented the discipline, and though skilful professionally, he was sullen, and worked no harder than in the Mediterranean trade. He did not repay the kindness of Captain Carteret, which was not only ungrateful but foolish.

The captain's clerk, James Mitchell, a plausible young man who was secretly an atheist and freethinker, noticed that Newton still had some religious opinions and a conscience, and set out to change his thinking. They argued and discussed during off-duty hours when on patrol in the North Sea, with one sharp action when they captured a French frigate.

Newton was shocked at first by Mitchell's amused dismissal of conscience, eternity and divine judgement. But he pointed him along a path he had itched to travel. Self-will and growing sensuality had long chafed at the restraints of his mother's Christian faith and morals. If Mitchell were right, Newton would be released, body and soul: free to indulge sexual appetites that would no longer be sin to him, and free to believe any creed or none.

At length there came a day, somewhere off the coast of Norway that early summer of 1744, when John Newton dropped his faith overboard. Outwardly, he became a militant atheist. Inwardly, his conscience still wrestled, but in time, 'I believed my own lie... Like an unwary sailor who quits his port just before a rising storm, I renounced the hopes and comforts of the gospel at the very time when every other comfort was about to fail me.'

This 'rising storm', this loss of all comfort, he brought on his own head. The innocent cause was Polly Catlett.

One morning in April 1745, while HMS *Harwich* lay in

Plymouth Sound repairing storm damage, the captain paraded all hands to witness punishment for desertion.

Two marines brought up midshipman Newton. They stripped him and tied him to the gratings. After the captain had read the articles of war, the bosun's mate flogged Newton's bare back with the cat o' nine tails of knotted ropes. The captain then announced that he had reduced the midshipman's rank to that of ordinary seaman.

The *Harwich* had been ordered to the East Indies and would be away five years. Earlier, when anchored off Deal, Carteret had granted Newton twenty-four hours to ride to Chatham for Polly's farewell, and Newton had badly overstayed his leave. He thus forfeited Carteret's trust. They had sailed down the Channel and joined a squadron escorting Guineamen bound for West Africa, but ran into a violent gale. Their commodore ordered his battered squadron and convoy back to Plymouth Sound.

Newton then heard that his father was at Dartmouth not far away, inspecting damaged ships of the Africa Company; surely he would find a way of exchanging him into the Guinea service if only he could implore him face to face. Carteret refused him leave, a midshipman who had abused his kindness. A day or two later, the captain ordered him to take the longboat to collect supplies from Plymouth quay; several men having already deserted, he had to ensure that all his crew returned.

At the quay, Newton suddenly decided to throw caution and duty to the winds. He slipped aside and walked out of the Royal Navy for ever—or so he thought.

Nearing Dartmouth, he was arrested as a deserter and marched back in irons to Plymouth, one of a motley set of rascals, to be flogged and have his rank reduced. Newton furiously meditated revenge, even murder. On the voyage south, 'My breast was filled with the most excruciating passions, eager desire, bitter rage and black despair. Every hour exposed me to some new insult or hardship, with no hope of relief or mitigation, no friend to take my part or to listen to my complaint.'

Worst of all was the loss of Polly.

At first light on 9 May 1745, at Funchal Roads off Madeira, an exhausted Newton slept right through the bosun's whistle. The petty officers had worked Newton harder than any.

The midshipman of the watch shook him awake with a friendly jest, as they had been special friends. Newton insolently dallied. The midshipman cut the hammock's ropes. Newton fell heavily on his still-sore back. In mute fury, he dressed and went on deck. He saw a boat bobbing below the side and a messmate about to drop down his bundle, who said that the captain had pressed two skilled hands from a merchantman and was discharging two ordinary seamen to the Guinea ship in exchange.

Newton's heart burned. He ran to the lieutenants and entreated them to plead with the captain that he be the other seaman. They had secretly pitied his flogging and expulsion from the quarterdeck and went to Captain Carteret. Carteret agreed, although at Plymouth he had refused the same request from Admiral Medley on Captain Newton's behalf: desertion must never be seen to pay.

Had Newton come on deck a few moments later the chance would have gone. Once again an extraordinary coincidence had shaped his life. But it had a disastrous effect on his character. As a seaman on *Harwich* he had kept his animal instincts in check out of pride. He would now be among strangers.

I rejoiced in the exchange ... that I now might be as abandoned as I pleased, without any control.

Newton, recalling 1745

From slaver to slave

Y ears later Newton could distinctly recall, 'that while I was passing from the one ship to the other, this was one reason why I rejoiced in the exchange ... that I now might be as abandoned as I pleased, without any control.' He was a few weeks short of his twentieth birthday.

He went on board the Guinea ship, the *Pegasus*, whose master, Captain Guy Penrose, exclaimed that he knew his father, and made Newton a steward. The future looked assured, for the *Pegasus* was in the triangular slave trade that carried Sheffield goods, cloth, firearms and trinkets down the windward coast of Africa to barter for slaves; then shipped the slaves by the 'middle passage' to the West Indies; and ran for home before the trade winds with a cargo of sugar and rum. Any captain or mate had a good livelihood, while a landsman who superintended a 'factory' could make his fortune, like their passenger Amos Clow, the ship's part-owner.

Thus Newton became a slaver. For the next six months of 1745 he sailed from river mouth to river mouth, down the coast and back, while Clow and the captain bargained with chiefs and factors for the slaves they had collected in their warehouses.

The crew always received slaves on board as enemies who would attempt to regain liberty. They were branded and put in irons. About a third of a cargo was female. As black women and girls came on board, naked, trembling, terrified, almost exhausted with cold, fatigue and hunger, they were exposed to wanton rudeness and divided on the spot for future use.

John Newton now let lust run unchecked. His heart was with Polly but his body refused to be denied. Opportunity to gratify his lust came easily, during the day as well as at night.

Newton said long afterwards that the slave trade effaced the moral sense, robbed the heart of every gentle and humane disposition and hardened it like steel. Unconsciously though, he was storing up vital evidence that one day would be decisive.

He was now not only a thoroughgoing womanizer but also a militant atheist who ridiculed faith and morals, and took special delight in destroying any vestiges of religion in the crew. Captain Penrose was not religious but he soon regretted the exchange he had made at Madeira. Newton grew careless, disobedient, even mutinous.

The captain's temper flared hot and so did Newton's. They flew into furious arguments. Worse, Newton made fun of him. Only respect for the boy's father stayed Penrose's hand. At the turn of the year 1745–46, when the holds were crammed with slave cargo and the ship lay in the Rio Nuna preparing for the middle passage, the captain died. The mate, Josiah Blunt, took command.

A nineteenth-century engraving depicting the horrors of the slave trade

Newton at once realized his danger. Blunt, who hated him, cared nothing for Newton's father and would take the first opportunity of putting Newton on board a man-of-war, and 'this, from what I knew already was more dreadful to me than death.'

Newton resolved to quit and to try his fortune in Africa. He asked Clow, who was about to land, to take him into his service. Clow agreed.

He was planning a new factory for the reception of slaves on one of three sandy inshore islands, the Plantains, south of the Sierra Leone peninsulas. Newton determined to retrieve lost time and be diligent, and the new factory thrived; it worried him not at all that his traffic was in human flesh.

Some months later they were trading for slaves upriver and had doubled their profit when Clow's former partner appeared. He found the market less attractive because of Newton and determined to destroy this new young Englishman.

One afternoon Newton worked on board the river boat

The Wilberforce window at Holy Trinity church, Clapham, in south London

sorting and checking; on this journey they did not ship any slaves. Clow was on shore, drinking with his crony. He returned at dusk in a fury and accused Newton of cheating him; his old associate had warned him. Newton indignantly denied defrauding him even in the smallest matter: 'This was the one vice I could not be justly charged with.'

Clow refused to listen. He threw him out of the cabin and, next morning, locked him to the deck by a long ankle chain as if he were a slave. Putting in reach a pint of rice for the day's ration, Clow padlocked the cabin, took the two blacks of the crew ashore and began to trade in partnership with his old associate.

This was the pattern of the next three or four weeks, a floating captivity on rivers and lagoons, thinly clad and almost starved. When at last they returned to the Plantains, the excessive cold and wet had weakened his physique and broken his spirit. But at least he expected release.

Instead, Clow took him to the forge. To Newton's shame and helpless misery, the slave blacksmith, while Clow watched, put him in ankle irons. Henceforth he had to clank and shuffle with two fetters linked by a chain, as if he were a slave. The head slave put him to planting a lime grove, of small shoots, to be placed in lines by the hundred, a backbreaking job. Like the slaves, he was made to work nearly naked, and the sun burned his body. Inwardly, too, he burned—that he worked under the orders of a slave, that he should be a 'servant of slaves' and the object of their pity. This, to a young white man of twenty-one in that period, was humiliation indeed. He kept himself sane by creeping out to the seashore in the brief cooler hour between work and dusk, with Euclid's *Geometry*, the one volume he possessed. He would trace the diagrams in the sand until, over several weeks, he had mastered the first six books.

One hope sustained him. When a European ship anchored off shore in answer to Clow's smoke signal for trade, Newton wrote a pathetic letter to his father, and the friendly house-slave who had secretly brought paper and pen slipped it into Clow's post-bag before sealing it. Newton told his father his dreadful condition and begged forgiveness and rescue. He sent letters on three occasions and wrote to Polly, too.

Not long afterwards another trader, richer than Clow, set up home on the island, which he left frequently to visit his other factories up and down the coast. Deploring the waste of a white man, he prevailed on Clow to give him Newton, who at once found himself decently clothed, well fed, and treated as a companion. The trader entrusted him with the care of all the domestic effects, to the amount of some thousand pounds, on next going away, and the 'sport and scorn of slaves' became virtually master of several until his new master, his new friend, returned to find him restored in body and spirits and his own affairs in good order. The trader appointed him to share with another Englishman the management of a factory more than a hundred miles away, in the Kittam district on the Sherbro River's southern branch.

They became close friends. Business flourished, in the usual way: not an article was delivered to the blacks in a genuine or entire condition, so that again, unconsciously, Newton was gaining vital evidence about the slave trade and the condition of the native peoples, whom he found honest and reasonably content until lives were ruined by the trade.

He again gave into his lust for women, acquiring a harem from the local tribe. He rapidly became prosperous. The local manners and customs grew on him. He enjoyed the upcountry trading trips. Within three months he had renounced all idea of returning to England, despite occasional pangs of regret for the loss of Polly or for the father he had wronged. He thought himself happy.

Far away in London, Captain Newton had received John's pathetic letter from captivity. He wrote at once to his great friend Joseph Manesty in Liverpool. Manesty had a ship, the *Greyhound*, not a slaver, about to sail to the coast. He instructed her master, Captain Swanwick, to enquire for John Newton wherever they traded and to bring him home. By February 1747, Swanwick, after enquiring up and down the coast, thought he had failed. But as he sailed close to the Kittam shore he noticed a smoke signal. He dropped anchor. A canoe approached.

Newton's fellow-manager had gone to the shore on the slender off-chance of a ship because Newton, about to travel inland, needed a few more items to trade; had the *Greyhound* passed only fifteen minutes earlier the manager would have missed her and she would have sailed beyond recall. He boarded her, and was asked whether he knew a young man named John Newton.

Swanwick came ashore at once. But Newton was indifferent. Swanwick promised that he should be an honoured passenger without need to work; he spun a yarn of a fat legacy waiting. Newton still refused. Then he thought of Polly.

Today the man is vigorous, and gay, and flourishing, and tomorrow he is cut down, withered and gone ... Ah, wretched guilty creature! Ah, stupid unthinking sinner!

The Christian's pattern

'Out of the deep'

C aptain Swanwick soon wished he had never rescued
John Newton. As they sailed slowly south, collecting
gold and ivory, beeswax and light camwood, Newton
gave no help to the small ship's company, either by his
seamanship or by his experience as a trader. Instead, 'My whole
life when awake was a course of most horrid impiety and
profaneness.' Not content with common oaths he invented new
ones. He tore at such shreds of Christian belief as remained in
any member of the crew. He ridiculed and parodied the events
described in the Gospels.

By January 1748 the *Greyhound*'s holds were full. Swanwick
intended to make the entire voyage home without touching
land, a navigation of over 7,000 miles. When they had reached
the North Atlantic, well wrapped against the cold of early
March, Newton amused himself by reading the few books on
board.

One happened to be *The Christian's Pattern*, a late
seventeenth-century paraphrase of the medieval classic by
Thomas à Kempis, *The Imitation of Christ*. Newton read it with
detachment as if it were a romance. One evening, sitting with
others in the forecabin, he picked it up and read:

Today the man is vigorous, and gay, and flourishing, and tomorrow he is
cut down, withered and gone … Ah, wretched guilty creature! Ah, stupid
unthinking sinner! How wilt thou appear at the tribunal or what plea
canst thou urge at the bar of sentence, to him who needs no evidence, but
is himself privy to thy most concealed impieties? Dost thou know this, and
yet go on unconcerned, how shalt thou escape the terrors of that dreadful
day?

A thought, unbidden, flitted through Newton's mind: 'What if
these things should be true?'

He suppressed it, joined in the general chat, went to bed and fell fast asleep.

Suddenly the force of a violent sea flung him awake. Water poured into the cabin, his bunk lay awash, and he heard a cry from the deck: 'The ship is sinking!' With instinctive reaction, he rushed towards the companion ladder to give help. The captain shouted down to fetch a knife. Newton turned to obey. Another man ran up the ladder, into a second great wave which swept him overboard into the night.

John Newton

They had no time to grieve, nor did they expect to survive him long. The upper timbers on one side had been shattered. Sails blew in shreds, the deck looked a tangle of cordage; the ship had become a wreck and it was almost miraculous that she had not foundered in those first terrifying minutes.

The man overboard left only twelve. Some bailed out the ship; others, including Newton, worked the pumps in pairs. Despite their exertions the *Greyhound* was filling. Had she carried a cargo of cotton bales, sugar and rum, or tobacco—or slaves—she would have gone down: the beeswax and light woods of Africa kept her buoyant but daylight showed that the rotting of the timbers in the tropics had caused them to leak in more places than could be counted. Men not at the pumps gathered clothes and bedding to stop the leaks.

At first, Newton looked on it all as rather an adventure:

pumping away, he shouted to his companion, 'In a few days this disaster will serve us to talk of, over a glass of wine.'

The other shook his head: 'No!' he said, and began to weep. 'It is too late now.'

By nine o'clock in the morning, four hours of relentless pumping had left Newton nearly exhausted, his courage seeping as he looked around at the wreckage and the slopping of the seawater. He went to the captain, busy in another part of the ship, to offer some suggestion, which the captain accepted. Newton turned away. As he did so, he said without the least reflection: 'If this will not do, the Lord have mercy on us!'

At once it occurred to him: '*What mercy can there be for me?*'—the ship's chief atheist, the loudest swearer, the man who mocked God's existence—'*What mercy can there be for me?*'

Newton stumbled back to his pump. Again and again icy waves drenched them, until with chattering teeth the two men lashed themselves to the pump itself to save being washed away. '*What mercy...?*' As he pumped, Scriptures long forgotten welled up from the bottom of his mind while the ship, broken and awash, plunged and bobbed in enormous, terrifying seas. He now dreaded death, for he thought that 'if the Christian religion was true I could not be forgiven.' Yet he remained only half-convinced that the Scriptures were true.

At noon he could pump no more and lay exhausted on his bunk for an hour until ordered on deck again. He was useless for pumping so was told to take the helm. For eleven hours until midnight, with one break for food, John Newton steered the ship. In the comparative calm of the half-shattered wheelhouse the past floated before him and it was not a pretty memory; above all, 'my unparalleled effrontery in making the gospel history (which I could not now be sure was false, though I was not yet assured it was true) the constant subject of profane ridicule.'

If Christ had really lived, and had risen from the dead, 'then I thought there never was, nor could be, such a sinner as myself.'

And he doubted that he, so long an opponent of God, could be forgiven.

At about six in the evening, when the last daylight had gone in those northern seas, the ship was free of water. Therefore they might survive. He thought he saw the hand of God displayed in their favour, and there arose a gleam of hope: perhaps he, John Newton, could find forgiveness after all.

He began to pray, although he could not pray in faith. 'My prayer was like the cry of the ravens, which the Lord does not disdain to hear'—an instinctive cry. But he wondered whether his cruel past was beyond forgiveness.

Standing at the wheel on that 21 March 1748, looking out at that dreadful sea, he began to think of Jesus, whom he had so often derided. He recalled the particulars of his life, his death, and the cross. He recollected learning in childhood that Christ's death was a death for sins, but not his own: Jesus had died, 'as I remembered, for the sake of those who, in distress, should put their trust in him.' If it were true... Atheism had been riveted to his soul as deeply as the iron nails that held the timbers to the frame of *Greyhound*'s hull. He could not tear unbelief away at a word and throw it overboard. When, at midnight, he was at last relieved at the helm and went below and threw himself on his bunk, he *wished* rather than believed that these things were true.

The morning showed that they had survived the gale only to face starvation. All their livestock had been swept into the sea and nearly all their provision casks smashed and ruined by seawater, except for some cod caught for amusement and some feed for the hogs, which was a week's supply if rationed. They thought they had enough fresh water, as they did not realize that many of the casks had been spoiled, and they believed their position to be nearer Ireland than it was. Most of the crew forgot the storm.

To Newton, God's intervention looked obvious, and amazing. Yet he was the most unlikely person on the ship to receive such an impression. He spent all off-duty hours carefully examining the New Testament that they had on board, a depraved sailor struggling with his past, with his newly awakened conscience, hopes and fears. The sodden, battered cabin became a place of conversion, like St Paul's Damascus Road.

The more I looked at what Jesus had done on the cross, the more he met my case exactly. I needed someone or something to stand between a righteous God and my sinful self: between a God who must punish sins and blasphemies, and myself, who had wallowed in both to the neck. I needed an Almighty Saviour who should step in and take my sins away, and I found such a one in the New Testament.

John Newton renounced his past, and believed. Immediately he found himself freed of his ingrained habit of swearing. It did not return, even in the uncertainties he went through as his faith matured. Newton never swore again.

The stricken ship sailed slowly eastwards, day after day. Newton now took a full part in working the ship, as an experienced officer, but off watch he hid in his cabin. His hope was growing stronger. He prayed more easily. He dared to believe that God had a particular purpose in saving his soul and therefore would save his body too, and his companions. God had saved the apostle Paul—the persecutor of Jesus—to show the world how great his grace is; perhaps God planned to do the same with John Newton.

On the fourteenth day the wind changed and blew them softly towards Ireland. On the twenty-eighth day they landed as their last pieces of food were cooking. Two hours later came a gale that would have sunk them.

For the rest of his life John Newton marked every 21 March as the anniversary of 'that awful, merciful day.' Writing up his journal in the form of prayer, as he often did, he recalled (in 1802) how

that terrible storm surprised me when glorying in the same spirit of infidelity, blasphemy and enmity against thee, in which I left the coast of Africa. No storms could have touched such a heart as mine, without thy secret, powerful agency. We spent a month in fear—of sinking or starving, or being reduced to eat one another. But by the time thy good providence brought us into port, I was no longer an infidel or wilful blasphemer. I seemed humbled and thankful. But I was still blind to the gospel, depending upon myself; I soon relapsed.

He wrote to his father and received a warm, loving reply, especially as the *Greyhound* had been reported lost with all hands. Captain Newton had been appointed Governor of Fort York on Hudson's Bay and invited John to come as his assistant. John felt he must oversee the repairs to the *Greyhound* and sail her to Liverpool. They never met again. But the captain had called on the Catletts and Polly, and approved the match.

Newton, after his immoral lifestyle, hesitated to renew his attentions to Polly, such a pure young woman, now twenty years old, and instead approached her through her aunt, who replied that the Catletts would shortly be in London and permitted him to visit Polly. He took the stagecoach from Liverpool, was tongue-tied, and received cold encouragement; but Polly did not refuse him outright. He wrote from his stepmother's house a passionate request to be allowed to write, then walked all the way back, having exhausted his funds, more than two hundred miles through the summer countryside, including many hills which would be levelled later—walking perhaps twenty miles a day. After an agonizing wait he received a cautious reply from Polly: he could write.

Manesty offered Newton the command of the slaver *Brownlow*. Newton decided that he must first learn to submit to authority and gain experience in slave trading; he therefore declined, and sailed as mate (first officer).

The *Brownlow* nearly ruined Newton morally and spiritually. He had no one to encourage him in his new faith, he slackened in prayer, forgot to read his Bible and cooled his gratitude for past mercies, until by the time the *Brownlow* arrived on the Coast, 'I was almost as bad as before.' When the slaves were shipped and girls came aboard he gave in again to old ways.

And so it might have gone on had he not returned to the Plantain islands of unhappy memories. Suddenly he fell ill with a violent fever. As he lay wracked, throbbing, and thirsty, despair overwhelmed him as he thought over his behaviour on this voyage, and wondered whether he could hope for forgiveness again. Then he remembered that God was known as a Father of infinite mercy and tenderness.

Weak, almost delirious, Newton rose from bed and crept to a remote corner of the island. Between the palm trees and the sea he knelt upon the shore and found new liberty to pray. He dared not make any more resolves but cast himself before God. The burden fell from his conscience. Peace returned, and from that hour his health improved so fast that when he returned to the ship two days later he was well.

From them on, he was able to exercise self-control, and prayer became a habit. And the memory of that black time reminded him often in after years, 'What a poor creature I am in myself, incapable of standing a single hour without continual fresh supplies of strength and grace from the fountain-head.'

During the next six or seven months Newton commanded the longboat which sought out black cargo in creeks and shores, and villages upriver, wherever a factor or a chieftain had a body or two to sell. In 1749, the slave trade was an acceptable business so a sailor making his first stumbling steps in the Christian life would not think himself engaged in crime, though later he would be appalled.

When the *Brownlow* returned to Liverpool, having discharged their slaves in South Carolina, Manesty promised Newton a command. With his future assured he renewed his attentions to Polly and won her. They were married on 1 February 1750, and fell deeply in love, so happy together that Newton nearly lost his desire to follow God.

Manesty made him master of the *Duke of Argyle*, an 'old and crazy' vessel with a turbulent crew. He sailed from Liverpool shortly before his twenty-fifth birthday for a voyage of over a year, the first of his three as a slave trade captain. He tried to do his duty by the common sailors 'without oppression, ill-language or abuse.' When slaves attempted to seize the ship he did not punish them excessively although they were, in his eyes, villains.

He regarded himself as a Christian. He even held divine service for his crew on Sundays while the slaves languished in chains below; but whoever labels him a hypocrite must first imagine that this obscure young sea captain, almost alone of his entire generation, had consciously accepted the insights and convictions of a later time.

Yet it was the far-away Polly, not awareness of God, that kept him from rape. Between voyages they had happy times together, making each separation harder.

By his third voyage, as master of *The African*, he was hating the chains, balls, and shackles and whips but had not yet woken to moral disgust at what he would afterwards call 'this vile traffic'. Later he wondered 'how I did not start with horror at my own employment.' But almost no one had called into question a trade that had flourished for centuries. Universal custom and Newton's professional interest combined to keep him blind to the trade's enormity.

'I am sure,' he would say more than thirty years later,

that had I thought of the slave trade then as I have thought of it since, no considerations would have induced me to continue. Though my religious views were not very clear, my conscience was very tender and I dared not have displeased God by acting against the light of my mind. The numerous and continual dangers to which a slave ship is exposed had thrown me into an uncommon dependence on the providence of God; this gave me a confidence which must have failed in a moment, and I would have been overwhelmed in distress and terror, if I had known or even suspected that I was acting wrongly.

Nevertheless, though unaware that he was engaged in a crime against humanity, he was storing up vital knowledge of the slave trade. Alone of the abolitionists, John Newton had seen it from the inside.

Towards the end of his third voyage he was in St Kitts. He had crossed the Atlantic without a single death because the poor market in slaves in West Africa that year allowed him to give his captives more room. He had now handed them over to Manesty's agent and thus to the slave market, and was enjoying the social life of Basse Terre, which derived from the sweat of field hands, toiling in the living death of the cane fields under threat of the cart whip. At one such party Newton met a lively, cheerful sea captain in his late thirties named Alexander Clunie, who was not in the slave trade. Some 'casual expressions in mixed company' revealed to both that they, alone among their hosts and fellow-guests, had faith in God. They walked back to the quayside together and soon became inseparable companions whenever the business of their ships would permit.

Until he met Clunie, Newton had lacked a Christian friend who spoke in a way he could follow. He had learned something of his own weaknesses, had read through the Bible again and again, and books, but was confused about the gospel, and troubled by a fear of backsliding again. Clunie brought him to firm assurance, and showed him that the God of amazing grace was not just a distant Judge but a most loving Saviour. Poring with Clunie over the Bible in the captain's cabin of *The African*, under Polly's smiling portrait, with the harbour sounds of Basse Terre wafting in, John Newton claimed Jesus' promise: 'Lo, I am with you always.'

He returned to Liverpool a happier man but longing to change his employment. Manesty gave him a new ship, the *Bee*, to sail as soon as ready. Newton took his leave in Chatham and brought Polly back. The *Bee* was still on the stocks, every day's delay weighing heavy, like the bolts and shackles of his distasteful work as a jailer of men and women whose offence was to be black, and captured by their slave-raiding fellow-blacks, then sold and resold between blacks and whites until herded into the holds of the *Bee*. Newton did not doubt it an excellent job; yet he hated it, and wanted more than ever to be with Polly and to share with her his new faith.

At last, in November 1754, the *Bee* rode at anchor in the Mersey and in two days they would sail. He left his first mate on board and returned to his lodgings in the afternoon. Polly and he sat drinking tea and talking over past events.

Suddenly Newton fell insensible at her feet. She believed he was dead or dying. After about an hour, with the doctor summoned, he regained consciousness. But dizziness, headache and other symptoms forced him to resign his command. He never left England again.

Manesty knew that Newton longed to retire from the slave trade, and obtained for him, by a coincidence as amazing as any in his story, an important shore post as one of the two tide surveyors of the port of Liverpool, who levied customs and excise duties on each ship coming in on the tide and searched for contraband. Thus, shortly before his thirtieth birthday, John Newton became a man of substance with some sixty subordinates. When Polly had recovered from the delayed shock of seeing 'my dearest John' collapse at her feet they turned their house into a centre of Christian service, for she, too, now believed from her heart.

In London, while on sick leave, Newton had met and heard the evangelist George Whitefield, and when Whitefield came to Liverpool Newton helped him so vigorously that the locals nicknamed him 'Young Whitefield'.

He was still too tongue-tied to preach, but he was often asked to tell something of his amazing story. From giving his testimony he passed to expounding Scripture. He taught himself Greek and Hebrew, and pored over biblical theology in his spare time from the Customs, yet was startled when some friends proposed that he become a minister.

As he approached his next birthday he set time aside every day for six weeks to pray for guidance. On 4 August 1758, his thirty-third birthday, he surrendered himself to God for 'thy service in the ministry of the gospel.' That night he wrote in his journal: 'Now Lord be graciously pleased to hear and accept and ratify from thy glorious throne the poor imperfect determinations of my heart. Grant that what has been sown in weakness may be raised in power; that what has been transacted before thee in secret may in thy good time be brought publicly to light by the effects.'

As he wrote long afterwards to William Wilberforce (who was born just less than a year after the above entry, on 24 June 1759): 'Wonderful have been [God's] providential dispensations

in my history. He brought me from a state of misery, wickedness and blasphemy on the coast of Africa; he led me by a way which I knew not, and at length brought me to preach that faith which I long, in the spirit of Voltaire renounced, despised and maliciously opposed.'

Statue of George Whitefield at the University of Pennsylvania

Abolition! 41

The first years I was in
Parliament I did nothing -
nothing that is to any
purpose. My own distinction
was my darling object.

Wilberforce

The young politician

One cold morning in December 1758, the Archbishop of York, the elderly, idle Dr Gilbert, was in his London house, ready to attend the House of Lords, when his chaplain brought him a small packet of papers: a title to a curacy near Leeds in his diocese for Mr John Newton, supported by the necessary three testimonials from clergymen who knew this applicant for ordination. They were countersigned by Newton's own diocesan who could have ordained him but excused himself. Newton was waiting in the archbishop's ante-room to be received in audience, then to be examined by the chaplain. The testimonials affirmed that this former sea captain, now tide surveyor, was 'apt and meet' by his way of life and his learning.

The archbishop, however, had heard that the man was an enthusiast who had vigorously helped George Whitefield on his preaching visit to Liverpool. The chaplain came out to tell Newton in softest tones that His Grace had to stick to the rules and therefore could not ordain him because he held no degree from Oxford or Cambridge. John Wesley, who knew Newton and his strong Christian witness, and also knew many ignorant and dissolute clergymen with degrees, was shocked. 'What a mere farce is this? Who would believe that any Christian bishop would stoop to so poor an evasion?'

For six more years, Newton remained a layman, and only Polly's sweet persuasion stopped him from opening his own independent chapel, which would have severely limited his influence.

Then, at the request of a friend, he wrote a long account of his evil youth and his conversion. The friend showed the letters to the Earl of Dartmouth, the rich young nobleman who had become an outspoken believer. Dartmouth wanted a curate-in-charge for his village of Olney in Buckinghamshire. The social importance of a peer was decisive. The Bishop of Lincoln ordained John Newton on 29 April 1764. That same year the letters were published anonymously as *An Authentic Narrative ...*, which became a best-seller.

Newton quickly won his parishioners' love. Unlike many rural clergy of the day he visited them frequently and regarded himself as their servant. Here was no cold, distant scholar or idle member of the gentry, but a roughened sea-captain-turned-parson; he was deeply serious in teaching and aims, but also had something of the quarterdeck about him, filling his unscripted sermons with anecdotes and nautical allusions, and his conversation with colourful sayings and touches of fun. He seldom wore clerical dress on weekdays, preferring to visit in his old sea jacket.

His articulation was poor and his gestures ungraceful, yet he held his hearers by the strength and passion of his convictions and the love that shone through his words. He used to say that the point in all his preaching was to 'break a hard heart and to heal a broken heart.'

And he wrote hymns for them. *Glorious Things of Thee are Spoken* and *How Sweet the Name* were first sung in the broad Buckinghamshire dialect; *Amazing Grace*, Newton's testimony in verse, was first sung after the New Year's Day sermon of 1773.

Newton's stipend was small and his savings lost when Manesty went bankrupt, but John Thornton, the very rich merchant, had begged him to accept an annual sum to be spent on hospitality and on relief to the poor.

When Thornton's half-sister Hannah and her husband, the retired Hull merchant William Wilberforce, had his fatherless nephew living with them at Wimbledon, they brought him sometimes to Olney.

This boy now became John Newton's ardent disciple, listening wide-eyed to his sea stories, laughing at his jokes, joining in his songs—and coming, as it seemed, to share his faith. Young Wilberforce revered John Newton almost as a

parent. The boy's mother and grandfather became alarmed that
he was turning into a 'little Methodist' and removed him.
Newton would send greetings to 'Master Wilberforce' when
writing to the uncle but as the years passed they lost touch and
Newton said sadly that nothing seemed left of young
Wilberforce's faith except a more moral outlook than was usual
in a young man of fashion. Newton did not cease to pray for
him and to hope that their paths would cross again.

Wilberforce's mother sent him to Pocklington School in
Yorkshire and then to St John's College, Cambridge, where he
became a bosom friend of William Pitt of Pembroke College,
and entered the House of Commons as Member for Hull at the
age of twenty-one. His charm, wit and friendliness made him
popular in London society, especially for his singing. In the
House he was a stirring speaker with great debating powers.
Pitt, now the youngest Prime Minister in British history, said
Wilberforce had 'the greatest natural eloquence of all the men I
ever knew.' Pitt valued his oratory so much that he once offered
to postpone the meeting of Parliament for ten days rather than
face the session without him. One parliamentary reporter wrote
that Wilberforce's speaking 'was so distinct and melodious that
the most hostile ear hangs on it delighted.'

In March 1784, at a crisis in Pitt's political fortunes,
Wilberforce brilliantly won the important seat of Yorkshire—he
became one of the two 'knights of the Shire' and an immense
help to Pitt. Yorkshire made Wilberforce a man of power and
significance who might one day become Prime Minister himself.
Welcome in the highest circles, privy to Cabinet secrets, the
closest friend of Pitt, Wilberforce had a future.

Then he was plunged into his own personal crisis. In the
winter and spring of 1784–85, aged twenty-five, Wilberforce
underwent a deep, long-drawn-out experience of conversion, or
rather, a rededication or rediscovery of Christ. He described it
as the 'great change'. He had invited his former schoolmaster
Isaac Milner, now a don at Cambridge, to be his companion on

a journey by carriage to the south of France. Wilberforce had not realized that Milner was an evangelical, and ridiculed evangelicals mercilessly. But as a result of their conversations and reading, Wilberforce returned to England in turmoil of soul, deeply conscious of his need for Christ yet loath to abandon his political ambitions or carefree social life. In his distress he turned to John Newton.

Newton had moved from Olney to the City of London one year before Wilberforce entered Parliament; and through the influence of John Thornton, Newton was now rector of St Mary Woolnoth, close to the Bank of England and the Mansion House; St Mary's was the parish church of successive Lord Mayors. Newton was amazed 'that one of the most ignorant, the most miserable and the most abandoned of slaves should be plucked from his forlorn state of exile on the coast of Africa and at length be appointed

St Mary Woolnoth

minister of the parish of the first magistrate of the first city in the world—that he should there not only testify of such grace but stand up as a singular instance and monument of it.' As he wrote to Hannah More, the celebrated playwright whom he had brought to faith, he believed that his case might be unique:

In the annals of the church of Christ few at the same age have gone equal lengths with me, in wickedness; few have sunk into equal depths of wretchedness; fewer still have been spared and reclaimed; and perhaps not one of these few has attained to preach the gospel, especially in such a situation as mine, exempted from want, abounding in comforts, honoured with acceptance and surrounded with friends.

But because Newton was despised and derided as a 'Methodist' or 'Enthusiast' by the world of fashion, Wilberforce was most hesitant in risking ridicule from his friends by seeking him out. At last, on Sunday, 4 December 1785, he went to St Mary's between services and handed in a letter at the vestry. Newton himself came to the door to receive it from this young man in a fashionable cloak whose face was vaguely familiar. Newton's heart leaped when he read the signature requesting a private, indeed secret interview. Wilberforce returned in half an hour for the answer. Newton never forgot 'the joy that I felt and the hopes I conceived ... From that hour, you have been peculiarly dear to me,' he told Wilberforce two years later.

A date was fixed for the Wednesday at Newton's home. Wilberforce walked towards Charles Square nervously before 'I called upon old Newton—was much affected in conversing with him—something very pleasing and unaffected in him.'

In the next weeks they were often together. Wilberforce dined at Charles Square; he took Newton down to the Wimbledon villa inherited from his uncle; he attended services to hear Newton preach, clarifying the truths and implications of the gospel; and was led to peace and assurance.

When the House of Commons resumed after the parliamentary recess, Newton assured Wilberforce that 'whenever you can call you will be a welcome guest. Great subjects to discuss, great plans to promote, great prospects to contemplate, will always be at hand. Thus employed, our hours, when we meet, will pass away like minutes.'

Newton stopped him throwing up politics for the church: 'It

Depiction of Wilberforce's December
1785 interview with Newton

is hoped and believed that the Lord has raised you up for the good of the nation.' Wilberforce wrote later: 'The first years I was in Parliament I did nothing—nothing that is to any purpose. My own distinction was my darling object.' What would be his object now?

Two great national needs came up again and again; one was the low state of morals and religion in England, especially among the upper classes. The other was the slave trade. 'My heart shudders that I was ever engaged in it,' Newton would say. His awakening had been slow. When he wrote *An Authentic Narrative* he had begun to doubt the lawfulness of the slave trade but did not attack it. At Olney, in touch with John

Wesley, who condemned it in a pamphlet in 1774, he grew aware of the swell of adverse opinion which was giving the trade a bad reputation, yet as something that could not be abolished without disaster to a nation's economy. By the time Newton came to London he was appalled that he should have continued slaving after becoming a Christian.

He preached against it, and was intense in his opposition to this crime against humanity. But the slave trade would not vanish because an ex-slave trader repented of his past. Only an Act of Parliament could bring in abolition, and no one could expect Parliament to stop the British trade while other nations continued with theirs.

God Almighty has set before me
two great objects, the
suppression of the slave trade
and the reformation of
manners.

Wilberforce, 1787

'God has set before me ...'

Newton provided the spur but the first signal for action came in the year of 1786, from Captain Sir Charles Middleton of the Royal Navy, father-in-law of one of Wilberforce's easygoing Cambridge friends and one of the only two open evangelicals in the House. As Comptroller of the navy he was chiefly responsible for its high state of preparation when the French Revolutionary War came. At the end of his life, as Admiral Lord Barham and First Lord of the Admiralty, he masterminded the Trafalgar campaign. As a young man he had won fame in the West Indies. The surgeon on his ship, James Ramsay, had become a rector in St Kitts until his care and love for the slaves caused the white planters to force him out. Ramsay was now Middleton's rector at Teston (pronounced Teeston) near Maidstone in Kent, longing to see the abolition of the slave trade—and of slavery. Both men knew that a trade considered so vital to the interests of the British Empire could be suppressed only by costly, radical reform and parliamentary action.

Ramsay had written two pamphlets against the trade and slavery. His rectory and

Sir Charles Middleton

nearby Barham Court became a centre for scattered abolitionists, most of whom were unaware of the others until they met at Teston, including Thomas Clarkson, who came for some months as Ramsay's curate. His Cambridge prize essay against slavery had not yet been published.

At breakfast one morning a harrowing discussion about the trade caused Lady Middleton to exclaim, 'Indeed, I think, Sir Charles, you ought to bring the subject before the House, and demand a parliamentary enquiry into the nature of that hideous traffic, so disgraceful to the British character.'

Sir Charles replied that the cause would be in bad hands. After they had considered other MPs Middleton wrote to Wilberforce. The captain read out the reply a few days later: that Wilberforce felt the great importance of the subject, and thought himself unequal to the task, but would not positively decline it; on his return to town he would pay a visit to Teston and consult.

Wilberforce did not meet Clarkson at Teston but received him with open arms when he called in January 1787 with a copy of his essay, now published. Wilberforce had now moved from his villa in Wimbledon, as it was too far away, and taken the lease of a pleasant house opposite the king's entrance to the House of Lords, 4 Old Palace Yard.

Clarkson called each week to exchange information and evidence. Wilberforce was making enquiries in the corridors of power; Clarkson was risking injury or murder in the slave trade ports. At length, sitting at his candle-lit desk, Wilberforce analysed their findings as he pored alone over the growing heap of papers.

First he studied the state of slaves in the West Indies. He found it bad. Then he looked at the harm to Africa. This disturbed him more. Then he examined the conditions for the wretched men, women and children as they were shipped—like bales, a black cargo—across the Atlantic. And he was appalled. The death rate on this middle passage was dreadful. Every dead slave meant loss to a slave ship's owner, yet hundreds were allowed to die every year at terrible humanitarian cost. Wilberforce hesitated no longer. 'So enormous, so dreadful,' he told the House of Commons later, 'so irremediable did the trade's wickedness appear that my own mind was completely made up for abolition. Let the consequences be what they would, I from this time determined that I would never rest until I had effected its abolition.' He was harassed in mind by warnings from merchants and planters that he would ruin the West Indies.

At a dinner party arranged by Clarkson in March, Wilberforce diffidently affirmed his intention to proceed, enough for Clarkson to alert his Quaker merchant friends, skilled at organizing petitions to Parliament. But it was during time spent at Pitt's estate at Holwood in Kent above the Vale of Keston, as they lolled under an oak tree with Pitt's cousin Grenville on 12 May 1787, three young statesmen in their late twenties, that the decisive moment came. 'I distinctly remember,' Wilberforce would recall in old age, 'the very knoll on which I was sitting near Pitt and Grenville.'

Under the oak tree Pitt brought Wilberforce's hesitations to the sticking point. 'Wilberforce, why don't you give notice of a motion on the subject of the slave trade? You have already taken great pains to collect evidence, and are therefore fully entitled to the credit which doing so will ensure you. Do not lose time, or the ground may be occupied by another.'

The oak stood for another hundred years, known as 'Wilberforce Oak.' Its stump is marked by a plaque.

Three weeks after 'Wilberforce Oak', the other campaign which Wilberforce and Newton had discussed made a great advance when, on 1 June 1787, King George III signed a 'Proclamation for the Encouragement of *Piety* and *Virtue* ...' Few who read it in newspapers or on walls knew that the moving spirit was the twenty-seven-year-old Member for Yorkshire, without rank or office, but determined to change the moral climate of the age no less, and thus to reduce serious crime. His motive was humane,

Wilberforce Oak

not repressive: too many men and women were hanged. Venality, drunkenness, and the high crime rate arose from the general decadence, especially the corruption and irreligion of the trendsetters: the nobility and landed gentry. The 'high civilization' of eighteenth-century England was built not only on the slave trade but on mass poverty, child labour, and political corruption in high places.

Knowing that many aristocrats pretended to be worse than they were because it was fashionable to be loose in morals and sceptical in religion, Wilberforce set out to change the country by changing the moral climate, making goodness fashionable, and restoring respect for the law in all classes. He had hit on an ingenious scheme.

The first proclamation of a new monarch's reign was always ceremonial, on behalf of 'the Encouragement of Piety and Virtue and for the preventing of Vice, Profaneness and Immorality'; a rather useless exercise except once, in the reign of William and Mary, when a society had been formed to promote its aims: a Society for the Reformation of Manners (in modern terms, habits, attitudes and morals). Covering his tracks by 'an amiable confusion' Wilberforce got the king to reissue his proclamation and then persuaded many bishops, dukes, and other notables to join the newly refounded 'Proclamation Society'.

When Parliament rose for the summer recess of 1787 Wilberforce drove along country roads and up avenues of lime and beech to stately homes. One noble peer laughed in his face. Another took him to an Old Master's painting of the Crucifixion as a warning of what happens to young would-be reformers. The movement caught on, beginning to give the upper classes a social conscience and an eagerness to help the poor. Even if some of the noblemen whose support he gained were notoriously immoral, Wilberforce believed strongly that the destiny of a nation could best be influenced by deeply committed followers of Christ, and that conversion to Christ was a person's most important political action, as well as religious. But vibrant faith was out of fashion. John Wesley had hardly touched the nobility and gentry. George Whitefield had done so, but his influence had been limited. 'Soon,' wrote Wilberforce about his own class, 'to believe will be deemed the indication of a feeble mind and a contracted understanding.' Wilberforce had to change that too.

On Sunday, 28 October 1787, Wilberforce, after church, took Newton back to Old Palace Yard for dinner and unhurried talk. Despite the age gap of twenty-four years and Wilberforce's high social position, Newton felt 'a peculiar friendship and affection for you', as he wrote a few days later, 'and I seem nowhere more at home, or more disposed to think aloud, that is to speak without restraint or premeditation, than when I am with you.'

They examined at length the progress and future of their two campaigns. Wilber, as his friends called him, had a third topic, but time ran out so Newton wrote his advice in a vast letter running to four close-packed foolscap pages in answer to the question: 'How far we may accommodate ourselves to the prejudices of those about us, with a hope of winning upon them, or at least of availing ourselves of their influence, to assist us in promoting those good designs which we cannot so well do without them?'

As for abolition and the remaking of England, Newton undoubtedly stiffened Wilberforce's resolve to proceed whatever the cost. For that very evening, 28 October 1787, after Newton had returned to his new home in Coleman Buildings, a short walk northwards from St Mary's and the Mansion House, Wilberforce took down his journal and wrote the words that have become immortal: 'God Almighty has set before me two great objects, the suppression of the slave trade and the reformation of manners.'

O my dear Sir, let not your
hands cease to be lifted up.

Wilberforce to Newton, 1788

Mr Pitt bows

Wilberforce's initial strategy aimed to secure abolition by international convention, since the British would not agree if other nations simply seized their share of the market. But his early hopes were dashed. Wilberforce and Pitt urged that 'petitions for the abolition of the trade in flesh and blood should flow in from every quarter of the kingdom.' Led by the town of Manchester, over thirty petitions had come by late January, and this normal way of conveying public views to Parliament took on a new depth of conviction and urgency. Liverpool, not surprisingly, petitioned in favour of the trade. Meanwhile, the press teemed with abolitionist pamphlets.

Wilberforce intended to bring on quite soon his 'motion in favour of the poor Africans. I perceive with joy,' he wrote to a constituent in January 1788, 'that their cause begins to interest the public, and I trust a flame is kindled that will not be extinguished till it has done its work... Nothing is more desirable than to excite such a general feeling against it as may render it *insufferably* odious; thus it will be attacked on all points, and so assailed it cannot but give way.'

Newton indeed suggested that the trade be 'publicly and solemnly declared contrary to right and reason, to the good of society, and the will of God.'

Pitt perceived more clearly than Wilberforce how the opposition would mount as the West India and the trading interests awoke. Recognizing that accurate information alone could discredit the planters and slave traders, Pitt ordered the Privy Council, by its standing Committee for Trade and Plantations, to investigate the slave trade and the whole subject of British commercial relations with Africa.

The original date for Wilberforce's motion, early February 1788, proved impracticable. He still hoped to introduce it within five or six weeks, although the passage of an abolition bill would be painfully slow since objectors had to be heard by their counsel at the bar of the House.

On 12 February, Wilberforce's two great causes leaped forward. Numerous bishops and peers attended the inaugural meeting of the Proclamation Society for the Reformation of Manners. Wilberforce opened the business, proposed resolutions and presided over the election of a committee. Then he and his great ally, the Bishop of London (Porteous) entered a waiting carriage and drove to St James's Palace for the first meeting of the Privy Council committee for examination of the slave trade. And here, day after day, Wilberforce had to brief counsel and members for cross-examination of witnesses.

One of the witnesses that first day was John Newton, now in his sixty-third year, distinguished in appearance and regarded with awe for his past history and present influence. The wheel had come full circle as the ex-slave trader took a coach to St James's Palace. He mounted the stairs, somewhat painfully because of a bad leg and other aches and pains, and waited in a long corridor beneath portraits of monarchs and princes, until he heard his name called. As he walked towards the open door of the committee chamber he saw, awaiting him, the Prime Minister himself: Mr Pitt bowed.

Wilberforce had suggested to Pitt that he greet Newton at the door—a great

William Pitt,
1759–1806

Bishop Beilby Porteus

honour. The Privy Councillors, the lawyers, and all in the room rose to their feet as the king's chief minister led in the former blasphemer and slave trader.

They now listened with rapt attention to his examination. Answering quietly, with no oratorical or pulpit flourish, Newton began his devastating exposé of the trade.

Then a new factor intervened. One week after Newton's attendance, Wilberforce was overcome by exhaustion, fever and loss of appetite. Sleepless nights and feverishness forced him on 23 February to consult James Pitcairne, the Scottish physician with such a high reputation in London that Wilberforce meekly went by carriage instead of sending for the great man. Wilberforce retired to bed. His former schoolmaster Milner abandoned his Cambridge lectures and fussed around, dearly loving to play the doctor. Wilberforce refused to stop work entirely, although as he wrote on Leap Year's Day: 'I … am still a close prisoner, wholly unequal even to such little business as I am now engaged in: add to which my eyes are so bad that I can scarce see how to direct my pen.'

Pitt urged him into the country air of Clapham, to John Thornton's, where Wilberforce had been given a room of his own since leaving Wimbledon. He returned next day, better, but under doctor's orders to drink the waters at Bath. Before he set out for Bath, he suffered a complete relapse: debility, loss of appetite, feverishness, and recurrent diarrhoea. The symptoms suggest ulcerative colitis, which is caused by stress. Seeing him wasting away, his friends sent hurriedly for his mother and Sally, his sister, and called in the eminent Dr Warren, whose opinion was: 'that little fellow, with his calico guts, cannot possibly survive a twelvemonth.' A consultation of the doctors produced an even worse verdict: 'that he had not the stamina to last a fortnight.'

Newton, who kept out of the sickroom, was convinced that Wilberforce would survive. 'Indeed,' he wrote later,

when you were at the lowest, my hopes were stronger than my fears. The desires and opportunities the Lord has given you, of seeking to promote the political, moral and religious welfare of the kingdom, has given me a pleasing persuasion that he has raised you up, and will preserve you to be a blessing to the public ... The difficulties and snares attendant upon your situation, makes me consider your afflictions, as especially tokens of the Lord's love to you, and care over you; and I humbly and cheerfully expect, that you will come out of the furnace, refined like gold.

The doctors treated Wilberforce with opium, at that time considered a pure drug with no moral question involved. He never became an addict but the prescribed doses, for the rest of his life, must have made him more muddled at times and certainly worsened his eyesight.

He spent his convalescence with his mother and sister in his beloved Lake District. Newton, working on their plans for chaplaincies in Bengal and the new penal settlement at Botany Bay, and waiting to give evidence at the bars of both Houses against the slave trade, wrote on 5 July that

I can honestly say, that were it practicable, I should not be unwilling to travel on foot, for the sake of spending two or three days with you in your present retreat. I have an enthusiastic turn for such a situation. I should not be very soon weary of the noble picturesque wildnesses of that country, if I was there quite alone; on the other hand I could rejoice to be with you, though we were shut up together within four walls. But to wander about from one changing prospect to another, to climb the hills, and to traverse the dales, in your company would be a gratification indeed! But I must content myself with imagining the scene, and the pleasure—and in this way I am often with you.

Wilberforce replied on 6 September, when his cottage was overflowing with guests, 'I believe I can truly declare, that not a single day has passed in which you have not been in my thoughts ... and in truth 'tis often matter of solid comfort to me, and of gratitude to the bountiful Giver of mercies, to reflect that the prayers of many of the well beloved of the Lord are offered up for me: O my dear Sir, let not your hands cease to be lifted up'; for his path was steep, difficult and dangerous.

Amazing Grace! how sweet the sound,
That saved a wretch like me!
I once was lost, but now am found;
Was blind, but now I see.

Amazing Grace by Newton

'I was blind but now I see'

During the little liberator's slow recovery, the ex-slave trader had forged one of the strongest weapons of the growing abolitionist movement: a short pamphlet with the title, *Thoughts upon the African Slave Trade.*

Newton's prestige as a veteran preacher, author and hymn-writer, backed by his extraordinary story, gave *Thoughts* a wide circulation. However much the fashionable world might 'deride or pity' his faith, it was compelled to face facts. His primary motive, however, was

a conviction that silence, at such a time and on such an occasion, would, in me, be criminal. If my testimony should not be necessary or serviceable, yet, perhaps, I am bound in conscience to take shame to myself by a public confession, which, however sincere, comes too late to prevent or repair the misery and mischief to which I have, formerly, been accessory. I hope it will always be a subject of humiliating reflection to me, that I was once an active instrument in a business at which my heart now shudders.

He gave a brief account of his early 'passions and follies' and how he came to the slave trade and engaged in it until the sudden illness of 1754 freed him from this disagreeable service.

Disagreeable I had long found it; but I think I should have quitted it sooner, had I considered it, as I now do, to be unlawful and wrong. But I never had a scruple upon this head at the time; nor was such a thought once suggested to me by any friend. What I did, I did ignorantly, considering it as the line of life which Divine Providence had allotted me, and having no concern, in point of conscience, but to treat the slaves, while under my care, with as much humanity as a regard to my own safety would admit.

He added that the slave trade was always unjustifiable, though its evil went unrecognized because of supposed economic advantage. But every plan for a nation's welfare which defies God's authority and laws is essentially defective and potentially ruinous. 'God forbid that any supposed profit or advantage which we can derive from the groans, and agonies, and blood of the poor Africans, should draw down his heavy curse upon all that we might, otherwise, honourably and comfortably possess.'

Newton described the region of West Africa he had known and then considered the slave trade, 'first, with regard to the effect it has upon our own people; and, secondly, as it concerns the blacks, or as they are more contemptuously styled, the Negro slaves, whom we purchase upon the coast.'

He pointed out the rapid and alarming loss of seamen—and potential seamen, since many died on their first voyage when still mere boys. Those who survived were continually exposed to the weather, to fevers, to the temptations of strong liquor and women: 'lewdness too frequently terminates in death.' Newton reckoned that at least one-fifth of those who left England for the trade never returned.

The risk of insurrections is to be added. These, I believe, are always meditated; for the men slaves are not easily reconciled to their confinement and treatment; and, if attempted, they are seldom suppressed without considerable loss; and sometimes they succeed, to the destruction of a whole ship's company at once. Seldom a year passes, but we hear of one or more such catastrophes; and we likewise hear, sometimes, of whites and blacks involved, in one moment, in one common ruin, by the gunpowder taking fire, and blowing up the ship.

When an insurrection was quelled the captain punished the ringleaders.

These punishments, in their nature and degree, depend upon the sovereign will of the captain. Some are content with inflicting such moderate punishment, as may suffice for an example. But unlimited power, instigated by revenge, and where the heart, by a long familiarity with the sufferings of slaves, is become callous, and insensible to the pleadings of humanity, is terrible! I have seen them sentenced to unmerciful whippings, continued till the poor creatures have not had power to groan under their misery, and hardly a sign of life has remained. I have seen them agonizing for hours, I believe for days together, under the torture of the thumb-screws; a dreadful engine, which, if the screw be turned by an unrelenting hand, can give intolerable anguish.

He knew of even more excruciating punishments, but spared the reader.

These were examples of 'the dreadful effects of this trade upon the minds of those who are engaged in it. There are, doubtless, exceptions; and I would willingly except myself. But in general, I know of no method of getting money, not even that of robbing for it upon the highway, which has so direct a tendency to efface the moral sense, to rob the heart of every gentle and humane disposition, and to harden it, like steel, against all impressions of sensibility.' He knew one mate, upriver in a longboat, who had bought a young woman and the child in her arms. When the child's crying kept him awake he 'tore the child from the mother, and threw it into the sea. The child was soon silenced indeed, but it was not so easy to pacify the woman: she was too valuable to be thrown overboard, and he was obliged to bear the sound of her lamentations, till he could put her on board his ship.'

'I am persuaded, that every tender mother, who feasts her eyes and her mind when she contemplates the infant in her arms, will commiserate with the poor Africans.' And many genteel ladies of England were shocked to discover the true price of the sugar in their tea.

But why do I speak of one child, when we have heard and read a melancholy story, too notoriously true to admit of contradiction, of more than a hundred grown slaves, thrown into the sea, at one time, from on board a ship, when fresh water was scarce; to fix the loss upon the underwriters, which otherwise, had they died on board, must have fallen upon the owners of the vessel.

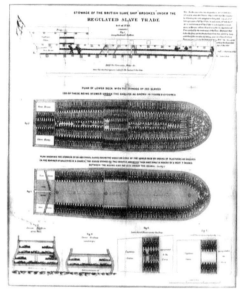

Diagram of the hold of a slave ship

He described the inhuman method of chaining the male slaves in pairs, 'fettered together, so that they cannot move either hand or foot, but with great caution, and with perfect consent. Thus they must sit, walk, and lie, for many months (sometimes for nine or ten) without any mitigation or relief, unless they are sick.' He described the three rooms of the hold, for men, boys and women, and a place for the sick; and how the slaves were packed tight in two rows like books on a shelf.

The heat and smell of these rooms, when the weather will not admit of the slaves being brought upon deck, and of having their rooms cleaned every day, would be almost insupportable to a person not accustomed to them. If the slaves and their rooms can be constantly aired, and they are not detained too long on board, perhaps there are not many die; but the contrary is often their lot. They are kept down, by the weather, to breathe a hot and corrupted air, sometimes for a week; this, added to the galling of their irons, and the despondency which seizes their spirits when thus confined, soon becomes fatal. And every morning, perhaps, more instances than one are found, of the living and the dead fastened together.

Epidemical fevers and fluxes, which fill the ship with noisome and noxious effluvia, often break out, and infect the seamen likewise; and thus the oppressors and the oppressed fall by the same stroke. I believe, nearly one half of the slaves on board, have, sometimes, died; and that the loss of a third part, in these circumstances, is not unusual. The ship, in which I was mate, left the coast with two hundred and eighteen slaves on board; and though we were not much affected by epidemical disorders, I find by my journal of that voyage (now before me) that we buried sixty-two on our passage to South Carolina, exclusive of those which died before we left the coast, of which I have no account.

He believed that 15,000 captives died each year.

When he had described the disgraceful treatment of the women (his own immoral past could provide evidence enough) he firmly denied the claim of hard-hearted advocates for the trade that

African women are Negroes, savages, who have no idea of the nicer sensations which obtain among civilized people. I dare contradict them in the strongest terms. I have lived long, and conversed much, among these supposed savages. I have often slept in their towns, in a house filled with goods for trade, with no person in the house but myself, and with no other door than a mat; in that security, which no man in his senses would expect in this civilized nation, especially in this metropolis, without the precaution of having strong doors, strongly locked and bolted. And, with regard to the women, in Sherbro, where I was most acquainted, I have seen many instances of modesty, and even delicacy, which would not disgrace an Englishwoman. Yet, such is the treatment which I have known permitted, if not encouraged, in many of our ships—they have been abandoned, without restraint, to the lawless will of the first comer.

As to the source of slaves sold by the chiefs, he admitted that many were convicts who had broken local laws, but most were captives taken in war; and he was sure that tribal conflicts often started because of the market for slaves. The traffic was not confined to the coast: many had come from the far interior; slave trading over many centuries had been disastrous for West Africans. 'They are considered as a people to be robbed and spoiled with impunity. Every art is employed to deceive and wrong them. And he who has most address in this way, has most to boast of.' And 'what an annual accumulation of blood must there be, crying against the nations of Europe concerned in this trade, and particularly against our own!'

When the ships arrived in sight of land, the men slaves were released from their chains

and their freedom from long and painful confinement, usually excites in them a degree of alacrity, and a transient feeling of joy: but this joy is short-lived indeed. The condition of the unhappy slaves is in a continual progress from bad to worse. Their case is truly pitiable, from the moment they are in a state of slavery, in their own country; but it may be deemed a state of ease and liberty, compared with their situation on board our ships.

Yet, perhaps, they would wish to spend the remainder of their days on ship-board, could they know beforehand the nature of the servitude which awaits them on shore; and that the dreadful hardships and sufferings they have already endured, would, to the most of them, only terminate in excessive toil, hunger, and the excruciating tortures of the cart-whip, inflicted at the caprice of an unfeeling overseer, proud of the power allowed him of punishing whom, and when, and how he pleases.

Newton hoped that the slaves were better treated now, and he knew of humane masters. But John Newton, with his detailed knowledge, must not be afraid of giving offence by declaring the truth about 'a commerce so iniquitous, so cruel, so oppressive, so destructive, as the African slave trade!'

We can no longer plead ignorance. We cannot evade it. We may spurn it. We may kick it out of the way. But we cannot turn aside so as to avoid seeing it.

Wilberforce, 1789

For abolition ... reformation

I n the opening paragraph of his *Thoughts* upon 'that unhappy and disgraceful branch of commerce', Newton had written that so much light had been thrown on it 'and so many respectable persons have already engaged to use their utmost influence for the suppression of a traffic which contradicts the feelings of humanity, that it is hoped this stain upon our national character will be soon wiped out.'

And so it seemed when, at about 5 p.m. on 11 May 1789, Wilberforce, though still feeling unwell, rose in his place to propose that the House consider the Privy Council report (which condemned the slave trade). He spoke for three and a half hours. Since most uncommitted Members vaguely shared the Enlightenment's rejection of slavery as inhuman, he had a

William Pitt addressing the House of Commons on the French Declaration of War, 1793, by Karl Anton Hickel

House predominantly friendly, yet uneasy, lest tampering with the trade should damage British commerce and ruin the British West Indies.

He knew that passionate arguments would not achieve his aim. He was not making a speech of protest before the general public, which counted for little in 1789; nor one designed to sway newspaper readers, nor a lecture for posterity. His audience was not a debating society but a body of men elected to maintain and strengthen British interests and (if they would admit it) the interests of their class, the men of land and commercial property. Wilberforce was on his feet with no other intention than to persuade a majority in this most critical and powerful legislature to take a particular action—to vote *aye* to the proposed abolition.

His speech created all the stronger impression for its moderate, unsensational tone, free from jibes, bitterness or pomposity; but his climax was stirring:

Sir, the nature and all the circumstances of the trade are now laid open to us. We can no longer plead ignorance. We cannot evade it. We may spurn it. We may kick it out of the way. But we cannot turn aside so as to avoid seeing it. For it is brought now so directly before our eyes that this House must decide and must justify to all the world and to its own conscience, the rectitude of the grounds of its decision ... Let not Parliament be the only body that is insensible to the principles of natural justice. Let us make reparation to Africa, as far as we can, by establishing trade upon true commercial principles, and we shall soon find the rectitude of our conduct rewarded by the benefits of a regular and growing commerce.

Pitt, Burke and Fox supported him but the House was uneasy. Wilberforce had to make the trade so insufferably odious that the House would vote for outright abolition. But—at Pitt's suggestion, and this was possibly a mistake—he ended by proposing twelve resolutions instead of a single, clear-cut decision, and the Commons turned aside.

Ten weeks later came the Fall of the Bastille. The French Revolution was one of the factors that ended early hopes of quick abolition.

———————

In the last days of 1790, Polly Newton died. Polly had never fully recovered from the shock of thinking John dead before her eyes in 1754. As the Newtons reached old age, still deeply in love, she had suffered nervous or physical disorders with increasing frequency, without losing her cheerful spirit.

In 1788, an eminent surgeon had diagnosed cancer. Polly begged him to operate when her husband should be away so that he would know nothing until it was over, but the surgeon warned her that an operation (without anaesthetics) might be fatal. She did not break the news to Newton until the following day that she would probably be the first to die, within two years at most. Shocked, Newton tried to face it in submission to the will of God, but 'strongly felt I was more likely to toss like a wild bull in a net.'

In the fifteen months remaining Polly spent much time studying and marking her Bible and her copy of the Olney hymns, and such hours as Newton could spare from his duties he spent in her room, the old ardour unquenched on either side. At one point she appeared to abandon her faith and turn against her John. Newton was thrown into agony of spirit yet refused to believe it was caused by anything but a turn in her physical condition. After a fortnight her love to God and to John returned in full measure.

'My dear Mrs Newton is in dying circumstances,' he wrote to Wilberforce on 23 November.

We have expected her dismission almost daily for about a month past. She is still living, but so low and weak, that she can neither move nor be moved, can hardly bear to speak, or to hear my voice, if I attempt to speak to her. It has been long a time of trial with me, for I am touched in a tender point. But the Lord is very gracious to me. I am supported. I eat, sleep and preach as usual. I see much reason to be thankful that she has been spared to me so long (more than forty years) …

She was uncomplaining to the last. In the final three days she was in a coma until on 15 December, John Newton, holding a candle close, saw her draw her last breath. He insisted on preaching the next Sunday, saying, 'Pulpit is my best physician', and he preached at her funeral. In thanking Wilberforce for his condolences, he did not disguise his grief. 'But the Lord's goodness in lending her to me so long (when I had deserved to forfeit her every day from the first) ought to affect me with gratitude and praise.'

As a widower he was even busier with interviews, prayer meetings and Bible readings, and drawing large congregations to Sunday sermons and weeknight lectures. When Wilberforce asked whether lectures might start later so that he and others could hear Thomas Scott at the Lock Chapel before coming on to St Mary Woolnoth, Newton regretfully refused: many people would be kept waiting a long time, having come early to secure a seat; the church was full before the service and latecomers stood at the door; and he must stop in time for those from outlying parishes to catch their last stagecoach home.

Newton did not write to Wilberforce frequently. 'If I wrote to you, as often as inclination would dictate, I should pester you with letters. But I consider your situation, and spare you— contenting myself with thinking of you, and praying the Lord to be your Counsellor, Sun and Shield.' He would tell Wilberforce of a good opening. Once a London clergyman died holding two separate livings, both in the gift of the Lord Chancellor. 'I need not tell you,' wrote Newton, 'of what probable importance it might prove, to this large, gay, giddy town, if these livings or either of them could be procured for a faithful minister of the gospel. And therefore I need say no more upon the subject.'

Rather than a flow of correspondence they hit on a plan whereby Newton would send an immense letter once a quarter, discussing their mutual concerns, including Wilberforce's 'persevering endeavours to abolish the slave trade.'

Newton assured him that it was not possible

at present to calculate all the advantages that may result from your having a seat in the House, at such a time as this. The example, and even the presence of a consistent character may have a powerful, though unobserved, effect upon others. You are not only a representative for Yorkshire. You have the far greater honour of being a representative for the Lord, in a place where many know him not, and an opportunity of showing them what are the genuine fruits of that religion which you are known to profess.

'Though we seldom see each other,' he wrote in another letter, 'I hope we often meet in spirit at the throne of grace. I cannot forget you there. I often commend you to the care, guidance and blessing of our great and good Shepherd.' Newton prayed that Christ 'may be the light of your eye, the strength of your arm and the joy of your heart.'

'But if God be for you who can be against you?' ... Go on, in the name of God and in the power of his might, till even American slavery (the vilest that ever saw the sun) shall vanish away before it.

'Wesley's last words', 1791

The long struggle

Wilberforce was now in his prime. This lovable little man with too long a nose had a marvellous smile and laughed a lot. Underneath lay a deep penitence, but his overriding quality was a sunshine of spirit. The poet Robert Southey wrote: 'There is such a constant hilarity in every look and motion, such a sweetness in all his tones, such a benignity in all his thoughts, words, and actions, that ... you can feel nothing but love and admiration for a creature of so happy and blessed a nature.'

A circle of friends and fellow-followers of Christ, including converts, grew round his informal leadership, including George III's first cousin, the second Duke of Gloucester, whom the Prince Regent hated for his moral stand and nicknamed (unfairly) 'Silly Billy'. Another was Josiah Wedgwood, the famous potter, with whom Wilberforce designed his celebrated 'tract': a Wedgwood piece with the profile of a Negro slave at the centre and the question inscribed around it, 'Am I not a Man and a Brother?'

His closest friend was his cousin Henry Thornton, MP for Southwark and a year younger than 'Wilber'. He was the son of John Thornton, Newton's benefactor, who had given Wilberforce rooms at Battersea Rise, the Thornton home at Clapham, when he had left Wimbledon—a country retreat from Old Palace Yard.

The cousins were opposites. Henry weighed a subject with deliberation whereas Wilber leaped by instinct, not always to the right decision. Distress summoned Wilber's immediate sympathy and he could be fooled. Henry, no less sympathetic deep down, went thoroughly into a case. In the Chamber or the Lobby, the Member for Yorkshire persuaded by graphic word-pictures; the Member for Southwark, by meticulous explanation. Wilberforce liked to consider himself a 'political

economist' but Thornton really was one, a
pioneer of currency reform.

They worked closely together in the
battle for abolition. Wilberforce's
early optimism was tempered by a
warning from John Wesley, aged
eighty-seven, written on 24
February 1791, the day before he
lapsed into a coma. The letter
was marked by Wilberforce as
'Wesley's last words.' 'Dear
Sir,' Wesley wrote,

Unless the divine power has raised you
to be as *Athanasius contra mundum*
[Athanasius against the world], I see not
how you can go through your glorious
enterprise in opposing that execrable villainy,
which is the scandal of religion, of England, and
of human nature. Unless God has raised you up
for this very thing, you will be worn out by the
opposition of men and devils. 'But if God be for you who can be against
you?' ... Go on, in the name of God and in the power of his might, till
even American slavery (the vilest that ever saw the sun) shall vanish
away before it.

Henry Thornton

Wesley died on 2 March. Seven weeks later, Wilberforce rose
again to ask the House to 'bring in a bill to prevent the farther
importation of African Negroes into the British colonies and
plantations.'

He had approached the debate in a spirit of prayer, looking to
God for 'wisdom and strength and the power of persuasion, and
may I surrender myself to him as to the event with perfect
submission and ascribe to him all the praise if I succeed, and if I
fail say from the heart, thy will be done.'

The subject loomed so vast now that he felt sadly unprepared, despite the months of study and cross-examining.

He spoke to the House for over four hours, basing his case squarely on the mass of evidence, and concluding with an expression of strong conviction that the country stood behind him. One MP recorded: 'His clear, circumstantial and plain account of this dreadful business and the whole of his strong arguments are urged with a peculiar gentleness and modesty.' He concluded with 'a most impassioned and emphatic appeal.' A great debate ended early in the morning two days later. As another MP had predicted: 'The leaders ... were for the abolition. But the minor orators, the dwarfs, the pygmies ... would this day carry the question against them.' Abolition was lost by seventy-five votes.

The struggle of the next sixteen years was costly. Twice Wilberforce was physically assaulted. Many denied outright any problems with slavery. A group of admirals claimed that the happiest days for an African came when he was shipped away from the barbarities of his home life. Most Members of Parliament feared change: such radicalism would threaten sacred rights, property, and liberties, not only in the colonies but at home. The horrifying events of the French Revolution and the slave revolts in the West Indies sent shudders down spines. As his campaign gathered momentum, Wilberforce faced opposition from planters, merchants, ship owners, the Royal Family, and the powerful ports of Bristol and Liverpool. One friend wrote to him cheerfully, 'I shall expect to read of you being carbonadoed by West Indian planters, barbecued by African merchants and eaten by Guinea captains, but do not be daunted, for—I will write your epitaph!'

In 1792 Wilberforce's annual motion led to a most eloquent debate and one of Pitt's greatest speeches. But the House seized on an amendment and voted for *gradual* abolition. When war broke out with Revolutionary France in 1793, Pitt, once hot for abolition, cooled off, putting national interests first. Friends tried to make Wilberforce cool off too, but he replied that, while in politics it was sometimes expedient to push and sometimes to slacken, as regarded the slave trade,

where the actual commission of guilt is in question, a man who fears God is not at liberty. If I thought the immediate abolition of the slave trade would cause an insurrection in our islands, I should not for an instant remit my most strenuous endeavours. Be persuaded then, I shall still less ever make this grand cause the sport of caprice, or sacrifice it to motives of political convenience or personal feeling.

The Revolutionary War brought much suffering to the poorer classes in England, as trade was disrupted, prices rose, food was scarce and unemployment severe. Wilberforce did all he could for relief and to steer a right course between individual freedoms and the need to protect the land from the revolutionary upheaval. His 'good works' included prisons and prisoners of war, hospitals and the poor, reforms in India and around the world, as well as in Africa.

A libel, painful to Wilberforce and quite untrue, that he cared for black slaves but nothing for white 'wage slaves', was put about by William Cobbett, the radical journalist. Wilberforce's contemporaries regarded him as always on the side of the poor, but the libel was repeated as if proven in a celebrated book of 1917 and widely accepted for sixty years. You can fault Wilberforce's judgement over this or that issue, but never his concern for human beings in need.

Wilberforce was also a great lover of animals and a founder of the Royal Society for the Prevention of Cruelty to Animals. His last surviving great-grandson, who was then over a hundred and blind, told me how his father as a small boy was once walking with Wilberforce near Bath when they saw a poor carthorse being cruelly whipped as it struggled to pull a load of stone up a hill. The little liberator argued with the carter, who began to swear at him, then stopped: 'It's Mr Wilberforce, I believe? … Then I will never be cruel to any of my horses again!'

Wilberforce's good works were very numerous, and he drew round him a 'cabinet' of others devoted to worthy causes, because a man cannot change his times alone. And he was sure that there should be no barrier between charity and faith. He taught, to the fury of the radicals of the day, that social reform must have a spiritual base, that reformers and educators who reject God will flaw their programmes and end by hurting the poor.

He was therefore strong for evangelism, at home and abroad. He subscribed to the new Baptist Missionary Society and helped William Carey with introductions. He was of use in high places to the newborn interdenominational London Missionary Society, and with John Newton and others founded the Church Missionary Society. He was a director of the Sierra Leone Company which, in a somewhat muddled way, settled ex-slaves in corners of the West African region where, long ago, John Newton had been a slave and a slave trader.

And Wilberforce longed to promote Christ among his own class. He thought out 'launchers', phrases or gambits to use at dinner parties to turn the talk to deeper directions, guided by his clear understanding of Christian truth and backed by his vibrant person- ality. In 1797 he wrote a big book

William Wilberforce

with an immense title, generally contracted to *A Practical View* (of truth faith as contrasted with its contemporary imitation). This became a best-seller. Sending a copy to Newton he declared:

I cannot help saying it is a great relief to my mind to have published what I may term my manifesto—to have plainly told my worldly acquaintances what I think of their system and conduct and where it must end. I hope also that my book may be useful to young women and others who with general dispositions to seriousness are very ignorant about religion and know not where to apply for instruction. It is the grace of God only however than can teach and I shall at least feel a solid comfort from having openly declared myself as it were on the side of Christ and to have openly avowed on what my hopes for the well-being of my country ultimately bottom [rest].

Newton read it from cover to cover three times in the next three months, long as it was, finding fresh inspiration each read. He wrote to their mutual friend Charles Grant:

What a phenomenon has Mr Wilberforce sent abroad! *Such* a book, by *such* a man, and at *such* a time! A book which must and will be read by persons in the higher circles, who are quite inaccessible to us little folks; who will neither hear what we can say, nor read what we may write. I am filled with wonder and with hope.

To Wilberforce he wrote that he praised the Lord, 'That a gentleman in your line of life, harassed with a multiplicity of business, and surrounded on all sides with snares, could venture to publish *such* a book, without fearing a retort either from the many friends or the many enemies amongst whom you have moved so many years.' He likened him to Daniel in the lions' den and Daniel's friends in the burning fiery furnace.

A Practical View, with the moral prestige brought by abolition ten years later, did much to ensure that Wilberforce and his friends at Clapham and elsewhere would change the moral outlook at a time when the British Empire was growing. Wilberforce had made goodness fashionable. Whatever its faults, nineteenth-century British public life became famous for its emphasis on character, morals and justice, and the British business world famous for its integrity. Most of those who ruled India and the colonies had a strong sense of mission, to do good for those they ruled—a far cry from the original colonizers.

The half-century after Wilberforce saw a marvellous flowering of Christian faith and a great number of applications in countless constructive enterprises. In the process, the Bible became the best-loved book of the newly literate. Christian attitudes moulded the British character, a Christian social conscience attacked abuses left by the more pagan age that coincided with the early Industrial Revolution, and Christian compassion relieved its victims.

O Lord, do thou guide us
right, and enable me to
maintain a spiritual mind
amid all my hurry or worldly
business, having my
conversation in heaven.

Wilberforce, 1806

Victory

Hard on the heels of the book, Wilberforce fell head over heels in love. Barbara Spooner was the third of the ten children of Isaac Spooner, one of the leading citizens of Birmingham, a rich, elderly banker and ironmaster. He had a house in Bath where Wilber met her. After a whirlwind courtship they married on 30 May 1797, the bridegroom thirty-eight, the bride twenty. Wilber's friends were deafened by peals of joy, and Hannah More said she had never seen a poor, honest gentleman more desperately in love.

Barbara was beautiful and amiable, though an attack of typhoid three years later spoiled her looks and she became nervy, fussy and overprotective. They had four sons and two daughters in nine years. Wilber was devoted to them all, however busy he might be in Parliament.

During those same nine years, 'the grand object of my parliamentary existence' remained the abolition of the slave trade.

Before this great cause all others dwindle in my eyes, and I must say that the *certainty* that I am right *here*, adds greatly to the complacency with which I exert myself in asserting it. If it please God to honour me so far, may I be the instrument of stopping such a course of wickedness and cruelty as never before disgraced a Christian country.

He had some encouragement. In May 1804, he secured the House's leave to bring in yet another abolition bill by the surprisingly high majority of seventy-five. Newton, deaf and almost blind, rushed off a scrawl:

Though I can scarcely see the paper before me, I must attempt to express my thankfulness to the Lord, and to offer my congratulations to you for the success which he has so far been pleased to give to your unwearied endeavours for the abolition of the slave trade, which I have considered as

a millstone, sufficient, of itself sufficient, to sink such an enlightened and
highly favoured nation as ours to the bottom of the sea.

The high vote was new proof 'that to prayer, faith and patient
perseverance, all things are possible.'

Wilberforce replied at once to his aged friend:

O my dear sir, it is refreshing to me to turn away my eye from the vanities
with which it is surrounded, and to fix it on you, who appear in some sort
to be already (like Moses descending from the mount) enlightened with
the beams of that blessed day which is beginning to rise on you, as you
approach to the very boundaries of this world's horizon... Pray for us, my
dear sir, that we also may be enabled to hold on our way and at last to
join with you in the shout of victory.

The bill passed its third reading but the Cabinet told
Wilberforce that he must wait a year. Meanwhile, news of
progress in America came from the future President Monroe. In
reply, Wilberforce praised the United States that 'without
having had so much light thrown on the subject as has been cast
on it here, you have seen enough to induce you to do your
utmost to put a stop to this unjust traffic.' The two men met,
and remained friends.

But Wilberforce was opposed by the Royal Family except the
Duke of Gloucester, and most of the Cabinet; by powerful
vested interests; and by many of England's heroes. In the early
stages of the Trafalgar campaign Admiral Lord Nelson, who
knew the West Indies well, wrote to a friend from HMS *Victory*
off Antigua on 11 June 1805 that he would not allow the rights
of the plantation owners to be infringed 'while I have an arm to
fight in their defence or a tongue to launch my voice against the
damnable doctrine of Wilberforce and his hypocritical allies; I
hope my berth in heaven will be as exalted as his, who would
certainly cause the murder of all our friends and fellow-subjects
in the colonies.'

Yet within three months after Trafalgar, the prospects for abolition grew brighter.

The death of Pitt in January 1806 was a deep grief to Wilberforce but led to the coalition of Lord Grenville as Prime Minister (Grenville of the 'Wilberforce Oak') and Charles James Fox as Foreign Secretary, in the Ministry nicknamed 'All the Talents'. Both were ardent abolitionists. The Cabinet included three uncompromising enemies of immediate abolition but in March 1806 Grenville and Fox agreed to Wilberforce's intention to put down, once again, a motion for general abolition.

He was about to cross Old Palace Yard to the clerk's office to give his required notice for the motion when James Stephen called, bringing a revolutionary idea: Abolition could be promoted as a vital aid to winning the Napoleonic War.

Stephen was a brilliant maritime lawyer, at first in the West Indies, where he conceived a deep hatred of slavery and the slave trade, and now in London. A widower, he had married Wilberforce's widowed sister, Sally, and the brothers-in-law had become great friends. In 1805, Stephen had written a short book to argue that a nation engaged in war held the right to search neutrals on the high seas and to condemn cargoes bound for hostile territory. He had convinced his readers that Britain might strangle any trade carried in neutral ships for the benefit of her enemies. Trafalgar, fought three days after he dated the preface, gave her the power.

The book barely mentioned the slave trade, but Stephen designed it consciously as a weapon for abolition. He knew that British traders landed slaves in neutral Danish islands for trans-shipment to enemy colonies, thus boosting the enemy's economy. If cargoes in neutral ships could be condemned, these traders would lose their profit and stop slaving. If slave-grown sugar and rum from enemy islands could likewise be seized, the enemy planters would cut production and need fewer slaves.

Pitt had brought in an Order in Council to forbid slaves being landed in newly conquered Dutch territory in the Caribbean.

Orders in Council could be confirmed by Act of Parliament. Stephen now suggested getting the new Ministry to bring in the necessary bill, and quietly attach to it all the prohibitions of an oft-defeated 'Foreign Slave Bill', that is: Slaves shall not be imported into captured colonies; no ship trading in slaves to foreign territories shall be fitted out in Britain or British colonies; and no British capital or labour shall be used for such slaving. Parliament would pass it as a war measure. And once so much slaving had been prohibited it would be easier to pass a general bill, bringing in abolition by a side wind.

Stephen could put up the suggestion; he could not approach the Prime Minister or Foreign Secretary. Wilberforce buttonholed Fox and wrote to Grenville. They acted at once, and brought in a bill reduced to barest essentials to ensure widest support. Wilberforce warned Grenville to present the bill on grounds of national advantage alone, to prevent a strong opposition forming on the 'mistaken idea that it rests on general abolition principles or is grounded on justice and humanity, an imputation which I am aware would prove fatal to it.'

On Sunday, 18 May 1806, Wilberforce could write in his diary: 'We have carried the Foreign Slave Bill, and we are now deliberating whether we shall push the main question. O Lord, do thou guide us right, and enable me to maintain a spiritual mind amid all my hurry or worldly business, having my conversation in heaven.'

Wilberforce decided to sacrifice the glory of proposing 'the main question'. If Fox did it, waverers would be won and enemies neutralized. Fox therefore gave notice of a resolution stating boldly that the slave trade was contrary to the principles of justice, humanity and sound policy, and that 'this House … will, with all practicable expedition, proceed to take effectual measure for abolishing the said trade, in such a manner, and in such a period as may be deemed advisable.' Advocates of gradual abolition could hardly vote 'No'. During the debate (10 June 1806) Fox made a great speech. Not realizing how near was his end, he said that if during his forty years in Parliament he should have accomplished abolition and this only, he should think that he had done enough and could retire from public life with comfort, conscious that he had done his duty.

Fox's resolution swept through by 114 to 15. Immediately afterwards Wilberforce rose to propose a Humble Address to the king, already agreed with Grenville and Fox, that the Crown

take the first opportunity of 'negotiating with foreign powers with a view to the *general* abolition of the slave trade.' Ever since 1787 Wilberforce had hoped for this, which would stifle the cry of the traders that other powers would ship the slaves and steal the profit. The Address passed unopposed. A fortnight later, on Midsummer Day, Wilberforce listened from the gallery as Grenville carried the Lords. Within days, despite the war, a copy of the Address was officially received in Paris.

Victoria Tower, Houses of Parliament today

The session was now too far advanced for an abolition bill to go through both Houses in 1806. Wilberforce disappeared to Lyme Regis, where Barbara loved the sea-bathing, to play with his children, chase his heavy correspondence and labour at writing a book of abolitionist propaganda which had been in his mind for six years but was written in a rush. *A Letter to the Freeholders of Yorkshire* appeared only just in time but had a powerful effect.

The death of Fox; a general election won handsomely by the Ministry; and an unfortunate though well-meaning diversion by Grenville, which was stopped with difficulty, made the last months of 1806 tumultuous for Wilberforce as he and his friends prepared for the climax of abolition.

Grenville boldly reversed the usual procedure and launched abolition in the Lords, at the start of the session, by a short bill simply abolishing the slave trade and declaring that to engage in it was a misdemeanour (changed later to felony). The bill was read a first time on 2 January 1807.

News came from America that Congress had brought in an abolition bill, with death the penalty, which now was in committee 'without opposition nor was any anticipated.' To James Monroe, Wilberforce wrote of his joy at the 'concurrence of our two countries in carrying into execution this great work of beneficence.' Success for Grenville's bill was assured by the evening of Thursday, 5 February. Wilberforce went to the gallery of the House of Lords and listened to the entire debate.

Grenville, who had no reputation for eloquence, began with the argument that abolition would save the planters from ruining themselves by overproduction. But even if further imports of slaves, by allowing a vastly increased acreage, should bring them profit, 'is it to be endured that this detestable traffic is to be continued, and such a mass of human misery produced ...?' He put the weight of his speech behind justice and humanity rather than 'sound policy'. His conclusion touched Wilberforce deeply: 'I cannot conceive,' said Grenville,

any consciousness more truly gratifying than must be enjoyed by that person, on finding a measure to which he has devoted his life, carried into effect—a measure so truly benevolent, so admirably conducive to the virtuous prosperity of his country and the welfare of mankind—a measure which will diffuse happiness among millions now in existence, and for which his memory will be blessed by millions yet unborn.

The Duke of Clarence defended the trade, while Wilberforce's young friend Gloucester commended the bill. The House sat all night, with Lord Eldon, former and future Lord Chancellor, strongly against the bill and England's leading Admiral, the Earl of St Vincent, declaring that since Grenville was a man of intelligence a witch doctor must have laid a spell on him to make him want to do such damage. The peers laughed but even among the bill's friends few believed that abolition would be sound policy, whether economic or political: all regarded it as an idealistic act of national self-sacrifice demanded by humanity and justice.

The peers divided at 5 a.m. and astonished themselves—and Wilberforce—by their overwhelming majority for abolition: 100 to 36, a majority of 64.

It was then that Sally Stephen broke her leg, slipping on an icy Clapham lane while going to a dying woman. Despite her nerves and feeble frame she dragged herself back, sent for the doctor and told the groom to ride to Westminster. Stephen hurried home in agitation to find her calm and comfortable. Her brother was much upset, but no one could spare time for Sally except the two little Wilberforce girls, 'and they cry by her bedside half the day.'

On 23 February 1807 came the vital second reading in the Commons. The bill was introduced by Lord Howick, Foreign Secretary and Leader of the House, the future Earl Grey of the Reform Bill.

Howick was an elegant though unimaginative speaker and rather hard of manner, but he put the case for abolition in able terms after starting ill at ease. He did not like Wilberforce and included no graceful allusions. Most speeches supported the bill. Enthusiasm mounted. As one Member sat down six or eight would be on their feet, including young heirs such as Lord Milton, Earl Fitzwilliam's son, as warm for abolition as his father was against.

The climax came in the small hours of 24 February, with the

candelabra in the Chamber burning low. The Solicitor-General, Romilly, who loved Wilberforce not only for abolition but for his interest in penal reform and the poor, swept the House to a pitch of excitement by his climax. He contrasted Bonaparte and Wilberforce each retiring for their night's rest: Bonaparte in pomp and power at the summit of ambition, yet with sleep tormented by the blood he had spilt, and the oppressions he had committed. And Wilberforce, returning after the vote that night 'into the bosom of his happy and delighted family', to lie down in pure and perfect felicity, conscious of 'having preserved so many millions of his fellow-creatures.'

The House rose almost to a man and turned towards Wilberforce in a burst of Parliamentary cheers, 'hear, hear.' Suddenly above the roar of 'hear, hear's and quite out of order, three hip-hip-hurrahs echoed and echoed while he sat, head bowed, tears streaming down his face.

I am truly thankfull for
Providence for permitting me
to see this great work
brought to a conclusion.

Porteus, 1807

Epilogue

A yes, 283; Noes, 16. Majority for the abolition, 267: an overwhelming vote. 'No one expected this great question to be carried with so high a hand,' wrote one of the ayes. '... No one is more surprised than Wilberforce himself. He attributes it to the immediate interposition of Providence.'

One month later, on 25 March 1807, in the dying hours of Grenville's All the Talents Ministry, the Royal Assent was declared in the House of Lords to the Act of Parliament which abolished the slave trade throughout the British Empire.

John Newton, blind and deaf, rejoiced that he had lived to see it. He passed his eighty-second birthday and lingered on, unable to preach but still a man of prayer, and died on 21 December. Wilberforce had fallen suddenly ill and could not attend the funeral on 31 December. He recovered, and for the next twenty-five years was a major force in British public life, even when extreme old age caused his retirement from Parliament. The abolition victory had brought him unique moral supremacy and he was tireless in promoting reform and compassion, and the spread of the Christian faith.

He gave much time and thought to the problems of enforcing abolition throughout the world, knowing that slave trading continued unlawfully in British spheres, and legally in other nations. He was indefatigable in efforts to secure abolition by France, Spain and Portugal. And he had hoped that abolition of the trade would lead swiftly to the end of slavery itself, that the slaves would become a free peasantry in the West Indian islands. When this did not happen he went to war again for emancipation until advancing years led him to hand over the campaign to Thomas Fowell Buxton. Wilberforce lived just long enough to learn, on his deathbed, that the Emancipation Bill would soon be law. He died on 30 July 1833.

1807 was a turning point in world history. For the first time two nations had passed a law which, as it seemed, was not in their political or economic interest but was needed to remove a great evil. As in every great battle, the victory was not total; much remained to be done, but all depended on 1807.

Perhaps a final word may come from old Beilby Porteus, Bishop of London, whose family came from Virginia:

Here then after a glorious struggle of eighteen years a final period is at length put in this country to the most execrable and inhuman traffic that ever disgraced the Christian world. And this Act will reflect immortal honour on the British Parliament, the British nation and all the illustrious men who were the principal promoters of it. I am truly thankful for Providence for permitting me to see this great work brought to a conclusion. It has been for upwards of twenty-four years, long before Mr Wilberforce brought it into Parliament, the favourite object of my heart; and it will be a source of the purest most genuine satisfaction to fill my mind during the remainder of my life, and above all at the final close of it to have had some share in promoting to the utmost of my power the success of so important and so righteous a measure.

Statue of an unfettered slave, at Pocklington School, near Hull